Author: Jacquie A. Jordan
The N.E.T.'s Effect Company
Canton, Michigan
Copyright © 2019
Printed in the United States of America

ISBN: 978-0-578-63038-0
Library of Congress Control Number: 2020903147

Contributors:
Editor: Dr. Shanna Smith, Assistant Professor, Jackson State University, Department of English, Foreign Language, and Speech Communication
Photograph: Lydia Kearney Carlis, PhD, Principal Photographer Eyemagination Imaging C-Suite Pics
Book Cover Design: Tyson Taylor, Louisville, KY
For Booking Information: www.journeytotheholycity.com
Email: info@thenetseffect.com

ACKNOWLEDGEMENTS

When undertaking a project that literally has taken many years to birth out, it is the support of those closest to you that helps you to keep breathing, keep moving, and keep pushing. Throughout this journey, my husband, K. Michael Jordan, has reminded me of our family Vision and Mission Statement.

We are evidence of God's love, power, and faithfulness, manifested in our worship, relationships, and stewardship.

Truly the ability to birth something so great must be preserved and protected. It is a gift that I do not take lightly but accept the responsibility to be a steward of this gift and share it with the world. Thank you to my best friend, supporter, and truth teller. You have made be a better lover, giver, and world citizen. Because of it, I can do my part in fulfilling our mission:

> *As God's evidence, we will magnify and glorify our Father in all that we say and do, worshipping the Lord with our whole mind, body, and spirit, communicating effectively with others, sharing God's love, having dominion over the gifts, talents, and resources, God has given to us to build wealth in service of God's Kingdom.*

DEDICATION

This book is dedicated to my dear friend, whom I met on my journey to the Holy City. She was the epitome of what it means to be a Christian and I will forever remember her smile, laughter, and voice, "Jacquie Darling, how are you?"

PREFACE

Pathways show our present, our past, and our future. We all take different pathways on this journey of life. Whatever course you should take, you can look back and reflect on where you have come from, understand where you are, and see where you are headed. I am on a journey and this is my journey to the Holy City!

The Holy City is symbolic to many people for different reasons. Ask the Roman Catholic, and they will tell you to come to Rome, which Italians call Roma. The pilgrimage to Roma is taken by many who bask in the glory of the great Roman empire and the vast historical impact of the Catholic Church. Whether it is walking the Appian Way or visiting Saint Peter's Basilica, there is a sense of peace, enlightenment, and understanding that a devout believer feels when embarking on this great journey.

Ask the Jewish man from Brooklyn his route to the Holy City, and he will lead you to Jerusalem, the City of David, or the Wailing Wall. This city marks the pilgrimage to the birthplace of their promised land, the birthplace of their faith, in hopes they may find peace and solace and make a sacrifice to the pathway of atonement.

The Muslim devoted to Islam will make his way to Mecca, otherwise known as the Holy City. To those of Islamic Faith, the Muslim shows his fidelity to the creeds of Islam in his pilgrimage to pray in solitude with those of like faith in the grandest Mosques that have been built by men.

Whether the Holy City is Rome, Jerusalem, or Mecca, the commonality is the desire for one to get to the birthplace of one's faith, a genesis. My journey was to a spiritual awakening in my faith, but was discovered in a place in the South, during my brief residency as a transient of Charleston, South Carolina, also known as the Holy City. Yes, Charleston, a unique city at the crossroads of slavery and Jim Crow; Charleston, rich and steep in aristocracy and wealth; Charleston, as I came to know it, was nicknamed the Holy City.

Join me on my journey as I explore the picturesque Holy City in all of its gore and glory.

Beautiful, breathtaking, awe. A place you must come to see. Are the people friendly as they say? Is this the land flowing with milk and honey? Will it be a place of peace and understanding? Will I find solace there? How will I get there? What adventures will I make on the way? Is there a lesson in this journey?

Finding the Pathway

Hello Jock,

I received your lovely letter. Jacquenita, I was glad to hear from you. Also, glad to hear you are back in school and everything is going well for you. I'm sorry you were having problems when I last saw you. You should try talking things over with some family when they get too much for you. We just might be able to help in some way. You would be surprised at how many of the problems you are having, we have experienced also. We are here to help whenever possible, but we can only help when we know the problem, or you ask for our help. We love you and want you to be happy. Granddad and I are fine. We went to church this morning and had a beautiful service. I'm glad to hear you are closer to completing your degree. You're right, it certainly is a blessing to have your tuition and books paid for. God is always blessing us; when we are trying to figure out how, He just makes a way. So always remember to put your trust in him and He will supply your needs. Like I always say, "Trust in the Lord with all thy heart; lean not to your own understanding."

Love, Grandma

Hmm, 'lean not to your own understanding'. That was Grandma's favorite scripture; she recited since the day I met her at eight years old. Grandma and Grandpa came into my life when my mom met and married their son, my father. I could be in class, just about to go to a party, or about to do something I knew was wrong and that grandma voice would pop into my head. After all these years I have kept my grandma's words in my heart, Proverbs 3:5-6. Funny how hindsight gives you a certain glimpse of 20/20 vision on what those words actually meant way back then. If only I had understood then, what I know now in my heart, and not just from my head knowledge "memory verse" standpoint.   I began writing this book in various stages of my own personal spiritual awakening as it is sharing the joy, pain, sadness, and comedy of the lessons I have learned in my life.

Since I was a little girl, as young as age three, I can remember my MawMaw and Pawpaw taking me on my first trip from Louisville, Kentucky to Dayton, Ohio. MawMaw was my maternal grandmother, and PawPaw was her husband. There in the sky on the big green sign, I sounded it out all by myself, "Sin –sa-na-tee, Sin-sa-na-tee, Sin-sa-na-tee. "Jockee, you sho are smart! There ain't nothing you can't do if you put your mind to it," said Pawpaw. Pawpaw was from Savannah, GA, and speaking a double negative was a positive as far as he was concerned. He knew what he meant and at age three I understood I could be Wonder Woman if I wanted to. He had a nickname for my cousins and I, from Rooster, to Geechee, to Rabbit. My nickname was Jockee. I was so excited I said it over and over again. Cincinnati, Cincinnati. It probably got on their nerves, but they let me do whatever I wanted. If only I knew that city would be my home by way of Columbus, Ohio, East Hazel Crest, Illinois, and Frankfort, Kentucky less than twenty years later. As we traveled, I remember seeing the Big Tall Balloon on a stick. It read: Florence Y'all. "Wow, MawMaw, what's that big balloon." I asked with a certain natural curiosity. "That's a water tower," she said. I still had no understanding of what that was then.

I had no idea that my own children would have that same question. I would explain it to them as they grew up in a neighboring county not even fifteen minutes away from that same water tower. For some years later, I would travel north on I-71 and pass the Water Tower on the left next to the mall. I later learned the history behind the water tower- that a municipality could not advertise for a privately owned business, Florence Mall. And so, they replaced the "M" in true Kentucky style with a "Y'". For years to come, for me, that landmark became a welcome sign signaling to tired drivers you're just minutes from the cut-in-the hill, a few miles from the emerging skyline of downtown Cincinnati.

I'm not sure if that first trip sparked my love of taking long drives or whether sitting in the back seat while my dad drove seemingly aimlessly Route 30 from Chicago to Mansfield, Ohio each holiday and every summer, stopping at all the quaint little towns in between. However, I acquired the taste for adventures of long drives without a map. That mantra somehow became the staple of how I would live my life, without a map for the next thirty-seven years. To this day, I take trips down the back roads of the Midwest and Southeast stopping in small towns to learn about their fascinating or most boring history. In college, road tripping was the thing we did when we wanted to get to the next party, up and down, across and in between Louisville, Frankfort, Lexington, and Richmond. The closest adventure was never farther than a car ride down a back road could take you. Once I moved to Cincinnati, I found my way by getting lost and learning the back roads to Dayton, Columbus, and Mansfield. I would just have a destination in mind, a direction I wanted to go and would just go, twisting, and turning, and getting lost. Some might have thought I had some testosterone in me because I wouldn't even stop to ask for directions once I started. I somehow fit that stereotype that men never asked for directions. I would just keep going, and somehow, albeit sometimes late, end up at my original destination. My method of driving seemed to be a thorn in my husband's nerves. "Why can't you just pull over and ask?" "Why don't you just take the main highway?" he would always grunt. I don't know if it was my father's influence, my own stubbornness, or stupidity, that I didn't get a map before I sat out on a journey. However, I felt sheer satisfaction when I would arrive at a particular destination, having found my own way. Whether intentionally or by accident, it felt good! I also felt confident in knowing if there was some catastrophe or natural disaster, I could rely on my excellent sense of direction to get my family out of harm's way. As long as you know your current location and which way is north, south, east, or west, I believe you can find your way. But what happens when you lose your sense of direction? The way I chose to navigate my journey was like making my own map out of a jig saw puzzle without knowing what the picture of the map looked like in the beginning.

If only I had understood the value of the words, "Acknowledge the Lord," that my grandmother instilled in my memory bank. Those words were so simple, but, yet so profound. How would my life have turned out differently? What choices would I have made differently? If I could have outlined my destination on a map, would I have taken so long to arrive at this place in my journey to the Holy City?

One thing I have noticed in my years of driving and traveling, is that you have to pay attention to the signs and as well as on what kind of road you are traveling. For instance, are you traveling on a road that leads to a dead-end, a one-way highway, or a two-way highway? Have you ever come to the end of a road and realize you missed the sign, you missed the yellow caution sign that said "Dead-End", "No Outlet,"? Have you ever missed the "Detour" sign or you took the "detour" and totally went off road? This has happened to me so many times in my life, when I traveled without a map. I would miss the cues in my life that would tell me I should be on a different pathway.

Have you ever been traveling behind an eighteen-wheeler truck and you need to know if your turn is coming but you can't see up ahead of you? There could be traffic, an accident, a natural disaster, danger. Because you are shielded from knowing what's ahead you just keep on driving until you are present with your reality struck like a deer staring at you in the glare of headlights. It would be nice to be able to have the warnings like we have with traffic reporting - accident ahead, road closed ahead, detour ahead, and construction ahead. All these road signs warn us to what is coming so that we aren't blind-sided. I believe in our life's journey, God gives us signs of things to come. The question is whether we are smart enough to listen to the warning signs we are given, or keen enough to recognize the warnings.

Come with me as I take you through my life's journey. Although, I have changed some names for privacy, the events are true as I remember. As you read my reminiscent memoirs of my life's challenges and triumphs, I hope you too will discover your map to your Holy City.

Part I

Following the Signs/My Compass

How in the world did I miss my twentieth college reunion? I mean I know all my sorority sisters are going to be there and they are going to have so much fun. It's just too bad I won't get to see friends I haven't seen in years, singing around the tree trimmed head to toe in pink and green, or tail gaiting until the Marching Band comes in at half time. I mean that's what we do. We don't even know most of the time which football team is playing. It doesn't even matter because the nostalgia from the camaraderie and laughs will fill the air as we reminisce and listen to each other recant stories of our life's successes, failures, and challenges since college. It is a bond we share, a sisterhood from knowing the truth of each other, no airs or pretense, just down-home black college family-style laugh-until-it-hurts reunion. There is just simply no homecoming like the aura, energy, and excitement you feel at an HBCU, (historically black college and university). And I can't believe I am missing it for a two-year old's birthday. I am not a happy camper right now. But the things you do for family to show them how much you really love them and care, leaves you hoping that they understand the sacrifice or will at least show some appreciation. I hope to tell my nephew one day that I was at his birthday party. I know it meant more to my youngest sister than she let on. So here we are road tripping it to Atlanta.

"Y'all sit back and be quiet. I don't want to hear a peep. I don't want to hear stop touching me, or when are we going to get there, or I'm thirsty. Not a word, don't even breathe hard! And absolutely no passing gas! Do I make myself clear?" "Yes, ma'am," ring in unison like the church choir singing, Yes Lord. Now, that's more like it. Peace and quiet and tall green pine trees. It is a great Saturday afternoon for travel, beautiful sky as blue as the ocean without even a single white cloud. We left a little late, but we should be there in plenty of time for the birthday party. At least I hope so.

Oh, my goodness, I think I just saw an alligator on the side of the highway. "Honey, did you see, that?" "No," Jordan said. "I saw it mommy!" That is just like our youngest son, Kevin. He is so observant. I think he would make an excellent scientist one day. "Mommy, do you remember you went with us on the field trip to the swamp and you and I got in the rowboat and an alligator came right under the boat?" "Yes Kevin, I remember getting back to the dock and you jumping out of the boat and almost capsizing it, with me in it! Uhm hum, I remember, even though I would rather forget."   I knew the mention of an alligator was enough to jar that memory in Kevin and we would be retelling this story over and over.   But this is South Carolina, and we had just passed Moncks Corner, so I guess it is not entirely hard to believe an alligator was laying on the side of the road.

I was thinking that I would get some sleep on this trip, but my husband is blasting the music so I will just shut my eyes and rest them for a while.

As soon as I opened my eyes, a little dim I yawned, "Jordan, you know this is the most dangerous stretch of highway on 26."   I can tell when my husband isn't fully engaged in the conversation, he just mumbles "Uhm hum," not providing any answers. This meant I didn't hear you at all. Just ahead of us, a man was swerving back and forth in the dark green minivan. I was thinking to myself; it is way too early for someone to be drunk.

But before I could get the next word out, our lives were about to change forever. "Honey, look out!" I gasped as the minivan, strayed over to the right and then took a sharp left sending the automobile tumbling over and over and over again, until it came to a deafening halt!

There was a dead silence, with only the sound of the zooming rubber tires pounding the pavement at 70 miles an hour. It's almost like it happened in slow motion. This is when basic instinct takes over, from the adrenaline pumping through your veins. I promise you I could hear my heart racing in my ears. My husband sprang into action and ran through the thicket until he found the car. I was frozen in time for what seemed like forever. In reality, it was only about 15 seconds. Dialing 911, I kept thinking surely someone sees our car stopped on the left side of the road in the grass with flashing lights. I just knew someone would stop to help. No one stopped. I was amazed that being in the South cars were passing us by. I guess that meant I was going to have to get out and help.

"911 what is your emergency?" "Yes ma'am, we are driving west on I-26 just passed mile marker 172. A man driving a minivan swerved to the right and then his car flipped in front of us. Please send someone now, please hurry!!!"

What happened next seemed unimaginable. I had on thigh-high purple swede boots and for a brief moment, I thought maybe I should take these boots off. I have got to run about 30 yards through a thicket in the middle of the highway. Then I remembered, this is South Carolina, I might need those boots to stomp on a reptile. I jumped out of the car, not even realizing my children were sitting in the back seat, quiet as a mouse, stunned and teary eyed.

I made it through the thicket which was a mangled mess of Spanish moss, pine trees and a burrow of grass with holes that looked like I was trespassing on some animal's home. No time for worry or fear, I had to be brave. When I made it to my husband, with cell phone in hand, I could not have been prepared for what my eyes would witness and for what my ears would hear.

The minivan was upside down, braced between the tree, and my husband who was holding it up so it would not move or fall. The man had been thrown from the driver's seat to the passenger side. His head and neck were perpendicular to the rest of his body. He did not wear a seat belt. He was screaming and crying and bleeding from the head. He was Hispanic and spoke no English.

This unexpected challenge was greater than my heart could imagine. It was no coincidence that the occupants of these two vehicles traveling west on I-26 would cross paths on our separate journey. In my spirit, I knew we were on that path, at that moment to minister to him. I remembered some Spanish, from studying with my children, enough to ask him his name. Angeles, he whispered.   His breath was pained and labored as I beckoned for my oldest son, Michael, a student of Spanish, to come. Then, I told him to wait once I thought about it.   If he came over, he would be leaving his younger brother and sister. So that was not an option. Instead, I would have to run back to Michael.

As I started back to the car, my foot was caught up in the wiry tangled roots from an overgrown tree which slowed me down a bit.   After a tussle and pull, my heel was free.   I asked my son how to say, "Do you know Jesus Christ?" or "Is Jesus Christ your Savior?" in Spanish.   I ran back with the notes on my phone. We prayed with Angeles, and he knew Jesus Cristo as his personal savior. We continue to pray with Angeles until the police got there. Wow, it had only been ten to fifteen minutes, but it felt like eternity.

As Angeles was air-lifted to the Medical University of South Carolina (MUSC) hospital, I knew there was a bleak chance for his survival. Later we would learn through the news media that Angeles had succumbed to his injuries. If there is any solace to his family it should be in knowing that when this tragedy occurred, he was not alone.

The somber ride to Atlanta seemed even longer now. I didn't need to tell anyone to stop bickering or fussing with each other. There is something about the realization of impending death that puts everything into proper perspective; where you can focus on what really matters. Embracing this moment of clarity, I thought about Angeles' family. The officer supposed that Angeles had fallen asleep and then over-compensated to make amends for the horrible mistake he had made. How many times do we find ourselves in similar circumstances where we know we are in a place of danger? We know we should have made a different choice; however, we could not change the course that we were already on and eventually we meet our destiny.

Riding in the car to Atlanta, I began to wonder how we got here and ponder over the many different situations I have encountered on my journey and how I have handled them. What signs did I miss along the way? What signs did I heed?

Danger Ahead

"Six o'clock news reporting. There has been a man canvassing the Newburg area in a white van. Police say to be on the lookout if you have any strange citing or notice anything strange particularly with the disappearance of young girl off Bashford Manor Lane."

"Mama, I can't sleep. Can I sleep with you?" "No Jacquenita, go to your own room. You have a nice room with Strawberry Shortcake everything: sheets, curtains, pillows, and rug. You are ok, go to sleep." I guess there is no way my mama is going to let me sleep with her. Since, my uncle moved out she liked her bed without me in it. I can't sleep thinking about Girl Scout camp. I like it but we take a bus from the school around the corner to the camp out in the woods. It is the summer, and when I go back to school, I will be in the fourth grade.   I will have to walk there in the morning. Oh, my goodness, why is that guy sitting in a black limousine outside our apartment.   He kind of reminds me of the guy on the Partridge Family, the big brother with long dark black hair. "Cookoo, I thought I saw a Tweety Bird, I did I did". It's my alarm clock. I must have been dreaming, I thought as I got dressed for camp. Mom was already in the kitchen making my favorite, two eggs over easy. "Eat your eggs," Mom said. Just then I remembered my dream. "Mom, I don't want to go to camp today. That man that's been on the news, I dreamed about him, he was in a limousine parked outside and I think he is going to try to take me. Mama, please don't make me go." "Jacquenita, I have to go to school today. You have to go to Girl Scout camp," she insisted. "But Mama, I said louder, "I'm telling you he is going to try to take me." Mama sighed and said that it was all just a bad dream. So, I got my sweater, stomped down the stairs and out the door. There he is! It was the same man, only he was in a Red Nova.   I tried to convince myself this wasn't real. Ok, I thought to myself, when you get to the corner, if he starts moving, RUN!   Sure enough, I got to the corner, and his car started moving slowly. Like basic instinct I started running. I only had one block, two driveways to cross before I reached the school.   The street came to a dead-end at the school where the camp bus picked us up. I ran as fast as my little legs could carry me. His car turned the corner too. He's coming,

I thought. Oh no, no one is at the school yet. Where is everyone, I'm early? Oh no, fear raced through my heart. Help! Help! I'm banged on the door as hard as I could. Loud music, glaring in the backgrounded, sounded like the black AM radio station. The Janitor came toward me with her light blue uniform dress that zipped up in the front. She was an older black lady with large round eyeglasses. I wished she hurried to the door. I screamed, "Help, Help, he's after me." As soon as she opened the door, he got back in his car and scurried off.

"Please let me call my mama! Can I stay in here until the bus comes? Please," I cried! I could taste the salt from the mixture of snot and tears. Whimpering and out of breath, I called my mom, "See, I told you, Mama, some man was going to try to take me today. I ran, Mama, to the school - the bus will be here in five minutes." Mama seemed surprised, "I'm glad you are alright, let me speak to the Janitor."

I don't know why a janitor was at the school since schools were out for summer break. But I am glad she was there. I never forgot that time that God warned me of danger ahead. At that age, I had no idea of the gift of God that lie in me, or that one day my own children would have the gift of premonition. People tend to discount children. But sometimes children speak louder with what they have to say then adults. One thing I have learned is that if God can make a jackass talk, he can bring a word from a child or anyone just to give us a message of warning on what lies down the road.

That was the first time I can remember having a premonition, an innate feeling that God was trying to tell me something. This was a sign of something to come.

This Road Curves – Slippery When Wet

"Ms. Shoulders take this note to your guidance counselor. He would like to speak with you." Oh, my goodness what did I do, I thought? I have been active in everything from gospel choir, to performance arts committee, Girls Club, journalist for the school newspaper, track team, and President's club. I wondered what Mr. Wilson could want with me? Could he know about the time I cut school with Ron? Oh, I hope that's not it. Maybe it was the fight on the school bus, surely Kayla didn't tell on me? My goodness, they had already told my parents! Did they have to tell the school too? It wasn't even my fault. Wow, home room was in building H, so I have about 5 minutes to get to where the administration was, in Building A. Time seemed to stand still when I looked at the clock on the wall. I could feel a drop of sweat bead up on my head.

"Ms. Shoulders, Mr. Wilson will see you now."

"Ok. Hello Mr. Wilson," I said.

"Have a seat Ms. Shoulders, I have been reviewing your file and I see you have taken all of your core classes and by the end of the year you will be finished with all of your core classes. Since it is October, have you thought about what you are going to do with your life?"

Ok, I took a swallow, before answering. College? Certainly, I had thought about it, but wasn't sure where to go or when. "Well, um not exactly, Mr. Wilson," I shrugged. "I know I want to go to college; I think I would like to be an Ambassador to use my French or a Journalist or work for the government. I might be an accountant; my Pastor's daughter is a Certified Public Accountant. That sounds nice I think?"

"Have you thought about what school you would attend?" Mr. Wilson continued his probe. It made me a little uncomfortable, but I managed to squeak out, "Well, my father went to The Ohio State University and the University of Cincinnati. I thought about those schools. A few of my aunts went to the University of Louisville, I thought about that too. Right now, my mom attends Prairie State."

"Ms. Shoulders, next Saturday, there is a tour of Historically Black Colleges and Universities coming to McCormick Place. I want you to go there and make sure you stop at the booth for Kentucky State University. This is where I went to school. You are one of our best students, and at Kentucky State University, I think you will have a great education and a great chance at getting a presidential scholarship. Take these forms and have your parents fill them out. You will have to score well on the ACT. That test is coming up in January. Take this book and start studying."

"Ok Mr. Wilson, I will try to make it down there."

As soon as I got home, I thumbed through the books, Mom would be getting out of class soon and swing by to pick up my brother and baby sister. So, I went upstairs and called my best friend Angela.

"Angela have you heard about the college fair that's coming downtown this Saturday?"

"Oh yes. I'm planning on going too!"

"Great, I can catch the bus to your house, and we can go together?"

"Sounds good, got to go!"

Angela was a member of the Girls Club with me and we had become great friends. She was Miss Fashion Queen.

She lived to dance and danced to live. Dance provided her an escape from everything else that was going on.

Mom came home with the babies and groceries. As I ran toward her to grab the bags from the back porch, I quickly spurted out,

"Mom, Saturday, me and Angela are going down to McCormick Place for a College Fair, and is it ok if I go?"

"Well if you can figure out how to get there and back before dark that's ok with me."

Mom had a test coming up and one semester of school left so she was really focused on that. In a few months, I would get my driver's license and that couldn't come soon enough for her.

"I'm going to take the bus to her house and her mom will drop us off."

Task one was complete, now to tell her about the truth of the matter.

"Mom, I muttered, I went to speak with my guidance counselor today, and he says I have enough credits to graduate in May.   I just need you and dad to sign these forms and $125 to pay for the application and test fee."

I should have known it wasn't going to be that easy, when Mom took two gulps of her lemonade and a long drawn out sigh. "What do you mean you want to graduate; you are only fifteen?" she scolded.

"Well, Mom do you remember when you grounded me for the whole summer last year, and I asked you if I could go to summer school since I didn't have anything to do?"

"Yes, go on," she said.

"Well I took my core English and Math classes in summer school, so I have no more classes to take."

"Well Jacquenita, we will let you know, in the meantime you can take the ACT."

I guess Mom never saw that coming. I can honestly say I didn't realize I would graduate early I guess I sort of ended up here on this path accidentally. I mean here were my choices: I could have stayed there and gone to the community college, or I could leave. What would I do there? Half of my friends were already pregnant, some of them were doing or selling drugs, or they were just all messed up. I had very few true friends, and this was my chance for change, and I wanted to take it. Mom wanted me to meet with the Pastor about my life. I was thinking; I mean really, it's my life.

Saturday came quickly. "Wow this place is huge, looks kind of scary." I don't see Ohio State University (OSU), or University of Cincinnati (UC). It was not like the college fair the school district had. The school college fair had mostly Illinois schools like Northern Illinois, Northwestern, Depaul, Loyola, Wheaton College, and Kennedy King.

"I think I will look at Howard, and Spelman too," I told Angela. "Angela, where are you going? "I heard about Tougaloo in Mississippi. I am going to go and talk to them," she declared.

"Toogowho?" I remarked. "Tougaloo!" She snarled at me. "You know something Angela, I don't think that's the right pronunciation. Anyway, I will meet you back here in one hour."

Angela knew far more about HBCU's then I did. Her church, Trinity was very Afro-centric and culturally sensitive. She spent most of her time there doing African dance.

Ok, well here it goes! I walked straight up to the booth; the guy there was the Student Government Association President. He was quite handsome too. "So, tell me about Kentucky State University?" Out of all these schools here, I think I like Kentucky State the best because I will be less than an hour from my favorite homemade chocolate cake. Yum, Yum, Yum. That's right- MawMaw's famous homemade chocolate cake was my incentive for choosing a school in Kentucky. I turned in the paperwork I had completed. The representative said I had a good chance of getting in. I just needed to do well on my ACT.

I took the Chicago city bus back to Angela's then on to the 96th and Dan Ryan so I could ride back to Chicago Heights, where we lived. The whole time I was dreaming of what school would be like. Prior to going to the College Fairs, I only considered going to schools like University of Louisville, OSU, or UC. When my mother married my father, he adopted me. All his friends from college became my aunts and uncles. I would pretend to be asleep listening to them talk about their college days. Now I had other choices to consider and it was a different world than what I knew. When I got home, I told mom about it and you know something, she never forgot what she said. "You still need to meet with Elder," she frowned.

A few months passed by and Mama reminded me of the need to meet with the Pastor. When Sunday morning came, as always, we went to Sunday School, church at 10:15, then dinner at the Purple Steer. The pastor managed to fit us into his schedule before the district meeting that night.

"Pastor, thank you for meeting with us. Our daughter has met the requirement for graduation and wants to leave. She just turned sixteen last month. We are not ready to let her go!"

"Bro. and Sis. Shoulders – you can't hold on to her, you will either let her go now or when you are ready to let her go, she won't go," said the Pastor.

So much for that, Mom thought going to the Pastor would give her a reason to say no. Instead, she became even more conflicted about the thought of letting me go. She thought about how I would find a way to go. It had been two months before we spoke of it again, until after I had taken my ACT. My parents dealt with things as they came. Mom's favorite response to just about anything that was more than two weeks away was "We will cross that bridge when we get to it."

I selected the boxes on the form instructing them to please send my scores to Ohio State University, University of Louisville, University of Cincinnati, and Kentucky State University. Finally, all my forms were completed.

 "Mom did you see my scores. They were really good. I know you and Dad don't want me to go. But, if I choose a school that's close to family, then they can look in on me." I could look in my mother's eyes and tell she was about to say something she really didn't mean. She had the noncommittal look like why are you doing this to me. She opened her mouth and said, "Jacquenita, we are going to sign your graduation application, but how you get there is up to you."

Ouch – monkey wrench in the program. I had not thought about how I was going to pay for college. I needed money. I went to see Mr. Wilson again. I spent the weekend thinking about what I would say on Monday to Mr. Wilson. I practiced my scenarios in my head, and finally decided to just tell him the truth. So, I walked into his office before the home room bell rang.

Mr. Wilson was walking with a walkie-talkie and pointing at something.

"Mr. Wilson, I know you told me to apply for that scholarship last November and now it is the end of March, but is there any way to apply now," I asked squeamishly.

"Ms. Shoulders, nothing beats a failure but a try. Come back after lunch and I will have a letter for your application. "

And just like that, when I came back, he handed it to me. "You need to mail this off write away," he said very matter of fact!

The letters of acceptance to the schools kept coming in. Every day it seemed I got another letter. That's great I guess, but I still had no money. Graduation was in less than thirty days and I didn't know how I was going to pay for college. I guess I would be working at the mall. Prom was that weekend and I went with Angela's brother. I don't know why this boy had my stomach in knots every time I talked to him. My parents didn't trust him. It's not like he hadn't given them probable cause. He graduated from high school early and did nothing but philosophize all day enlightening his mind. But I liked him. I liked him a lot! He made me feel like I was the most important person in the world. He was wise beyond his years but confused too. He thought I would forget about him when I went off to college. Back then, all I could think about is how he had my heart because he understood me wanting to go away to college. He supported me, he got that. I felt my parents didn't understand. "You are so beautiful, and smart" He whispered in my ear while I was taking my senior pictures that rainy day at the studio. Now here I stood at the crossroads, my mind clouded. "Choose the straight and narrow path" are the words I heard in the back of my head. "I want to show you something you have never felt; it will feel so good," is what I heard in my ear. I was led off the path and I easily followed without too much persuasion. Then I was busted.

"In my house! You are disrespecting me in my house! Girl, it's just two weeks now before graduation, and you have got to get out of my house. You think you are grown, then be grown and out of my house."

Mama didn't play any games. It was her house and her rules. When I set out to graduate early everything seemed so easy. Now I didn't know. My head was spinning. I thought, "I am going to go call MawMaw and see if I can come and stay with her after graduation."

I prayed, *"Oh my God. Please God, I know I haven't been right. I know I have sinned, but please forgive me. Please make everything right now."*

Funny how quickly we learn to pray when we get into trouble. Where was God when I brought that boy home to my mama's house or when I told a lie? Where was God, when I heard God telling me which path to take and still took the wrong path? But here I was in typical fashion needing a prayer answered and repenting. That weekend seemed like the longest weekend for a teenager. I couldn't wait until Monday so I could go to school. I went to check the mail that Monday when I came home from school. An envelope from Kentucky State University addressed to Ms. Jacquenita A. Shoulders was in the mailbox. That's me. I couldn't bring myself to open it. I must call MawMaw and talk to her, I thought.

The phone rang at least ten times before she picked up, "Hellar" "Hi MawMaw, it's me Jock." "I know who you are Jacquenita, what do you want?" "Well how are you doing? I'm ok, missing your Pawpaw, he sure was good to me."

I missed the opportunity to comfort MawMaw, so focused on my own problems, I continued, "Well MawMaw, you know I will graduate in two weeks."

She replied, "Yes, how did your prom dress fit?" MawMaw had made my prom dress for me, it was a tailored fit, and no one had my dress. But that dress was the farthest thing from my mind. I didn't want to be ungrateful, so I mustered up an excited exclamation,

"Awe MawMaw it was beautiful. Thank you."

"That was my graduation gift to you," she said. "Yes, well I'm thinking about going to Kentucky State University or the University of Louisville in the fall and I was hoping you would let me stay with you."

"You know you can stay with me, just help me out with a bill."

"Ok then, it was settled," I breathed a sigh of relief. "I am going to tell Mom when she gets home from work. Love you bye."

Since Pawpaw had died, MawMaw welcomed all company, if it was the giving or paying kind. She collected his pension and social security, so she didn't really want for anything, but if she saw an opportunity to get a new hat and matching shoes, with a pocketbook and hanky to match she took it.

Well, that went well, I guess, I would have to open this letter. "Dear Ms. Jacquenita A. Shoulders we are pleased to accept your application for admission. In addition, you have been awarded a Presidential Scholarship"……………….. "OOOOOh my goodness, thank you, thank you, thank you Jesus!" I repeated over and over. I couldn't wait till Mom got home. It was 3:30, she would be home at any minute. Just then she walked through the door.

"Uhm - Ma –" I said, as I handed her the envelope. She was happy but there was some sadness in her voice as she said, oh "That's good." I had seen that sadness in her before, when I was seven years old and stood next to her looking out of the window of our apartment in Robinwood one cold winter when the icicles and snow made it impossible for her to go to school or work. Looking up to her, I remember telling her, Mama, God would take care of us. This time was different. This wasn't Robinwood, and I wasn't seven, I was sixteen and I knew it was time for me to make a move, even if it meant leaving my mama. Even though I felt the sign said, "Slow Down, Curve Ahead," I felt like if I didn't take this chance and leap now, I would never leap again.

I left for Kentucky in July after the Taste of Chicago. It was extremely hot that year. I was excited. I was scared. I was ready, or so I thought. It's funny how the road wasn't the expected path. But, when I think about it now, everything happened for a reason. I was always moving toward the next thing, the next stop. I seemed to never stand still to simply relish the moment in time, always planning, and strategizing about what was next.

The Scenic Route

"Ms. Shoulders, Ms. Shoulders, did you hear the question?" "Sir, the answer is ....." And just like that, I rattled off the answer to his question, much to his amazement. He couldn't take off class participation points from someone sitting on the front row asleep, dare I say sound asleep, snoring, and who answered him correctly with a keen insight and understanding on the Bible. Dr. Rowe, who was agnostic, had that look that spoke volumes, "I'll get you next time". I nudged Leslie, who had her head in the books too! She smirked a half-smile that said, *I really need more than two hours of sleep*. We had been to Lexington the night before and all I could think about was sticking together. This was more about not letting anyone break your spirit. We were sisters unified by our common purpose. We had just one more day, and we would be full-fledged members of the organization. When I think about how I ended up going to the rush by myself, because my best friend went to a different rush, I knew I had made the right choice. What could I say- I had a 4.0 GPA, the look, leadership, and the attitude? The only thing I didn't have going for me is that I wasn't a legacy. In fact, my only acquaintance with this sorority was by writing an application for a scholarship back in Markham, Illinois. The few cousins I knew who were in a sorority either wore red and white or blue and white; together at family reunions they were quite patriotic. So how did I end up here? In the back of my head was always how I made the organization better, not how it made me better. At least from my perspective, being a member would not change me or my core values. I was supposed to be a foreign-exchange student that semester studying abroad in England. Somehow, in a twist of fate, my parents didn't turn in my passport paperwork – so I stayed that fall and was initiated as a member. Who knew I would make friendships and bonds that have lasted a lifetime?

Many a day, I thought about how I got to school in Kentucky and how I had applied for other institutions of higher learning and had even been accepted to some of them, but Kentucky State University had won my heart and what a colorful experience it was. I remember going back on the weekends to spend with MawMaw, sometimes speeding.

I remember driving one day back to Louisville, and a car, red Nissan Sentra sporty two door sedan speeding past me. It was raining that day. I was a bit perturbed as I slid into the other lane to narrowly avoid being hit by the red sedan who was pushing at least 85 on the speedometer. Ironically, it was the car that I wanted but I happened to be driving a 1979 Green Pontiac Grand Prix that looked like it would have been a sporty car in my parents' heyday. About ten miles before I hit Jefferson County that same car had flipped and turned. The driver died. That was the first time I had even thought about my own mortality even though I had at least three friends from high school who were shot and killed. This was a sign on my journey that I needed to think about eternity. I didn't dwell on the thought though. I skimmed over the idea like warmed over leftovers; it wasn't too appetizing to dwell on it, so I kept on living my life in typical haphazard fashion and sometimes following the cues and signs and other times just going rogue off the road.

It was a colorful scenic route that was full of folly, fun, and excitement. God continued to put signs on my pathway for me to follow. If I can say anything to parents, is that don't ever stop praying or give up on your children. Even when it seems they are on a dead-end street at the point of no return, keep praying. I honestly could feel my mother praying for me when I would be on the verge of doing something I shouldn't. If it wasn't for the prayers of my mother, surely my life would have turned out entirely different. There were some paths I went down that were dead-end but somehow, God placed there an escape route for me.

Bridge Closed Ahead

If you're reading this letter, then, I have left you all here. I am so full of pain. I am angry. I mean, how dare they come to the house and tell me what I should and should not do. I blame them and myself. I shouldn't have listened to them. I could hear a still tiny voice saying no, don't do it. That tiny voice just got smaller and smaller. I feel like I was tricked. I feel just like Pinocchio. You know when he wanted to become a real boy he did what the con man told him. And what did he end up – a jackass. Well I have really messed up now. And so, know that I love you all, but I can no longer live with the guilt or shame. There is no way God could ever forgive me. I'm so sorry. I'm so sorry.

I wrote the letter in pink ink on green paper and folded it up. I put it in my Green two-door 1979 Pontiac Grand Prix. As I drove to the 2nd Street bridge I wondered about the other women I had met. I wondered why were they there? Who were these teens, women in their twenties and thirties, and forties? Why were they there? I could still feel the cold room. It was over so quickly. I immediately felt guilt. I had been crying for two weeks. The tears I cried didn't take away my pain or the longing

I had. When Sunday morning came, it was a bright and sunny day in July. I had on a beautiful pink dress. I can still see strangers glaring at me. They don't have to tell me what I'm doing is wrong. So many other people told me what I was doing was my choice. As soon as it was over, I felt guilty. I no longer had the love inside of me. How could I have done this? How could I have gone down this path? I know now. The guilt and the shame I felt, there was no way God could ever forgive me. What I got for my choice was butter cookies and juice. Really? Yes, butter cookies and juice. I ate so many cookies to try to fill that hunger inside of me. That hunger turned to emptiness. I was all used up. Why couldn't I have listened to that voice? It was like all the other noises were louder than that still small voice. I never wanted to eat butter cookies or drink juice again.

"Oh God, I'm so sorry. Here I am at this Bridge on a Sunday morning. I know I loved you as a child. As a child I gave my life to you and it was so simple. I could feel you speaking to me and through me, even though I didn't quite understand how your Spirit flowed through me. But now life was not so simple. It was so much more complicated. I pushed to leave home at sixteen. I wished I could go back now and be that little girl. I have been gone only two years. I don't know where I

went wrong. I feel so low down I don't think I could ever get out of this pit. How could your love reach me? How could you forgive me?"

I thought, well I had made my bed in Hell, so now I may as well go sleep there. Just then there was a car passing. The passing car startled me, so I thought I would postpone my farewell a few hours. I know what I will do, I told myself, I will go to church and come back here. I will leave before the altar call and come back and finish what I have started. It is the only way.

"In the morning when I rise, In the morning when I rise, In the morning when I rise, In the morning when I rise, I going rise Holy when I rise, I'm going rise righteous, when I rise!" That was the song that was blasting on like a pipe parade during testimony service. I could barely hear my thoughts over the loud tooting of the saxophone, smooth sound of the trombone, clashing of the cymbals, and the thumping of the base guitar in the background. With each thump, I felt guilt. The folks were shouting and jumping everywhere. On a different day I would have been beating my tambourine the way my MawMaw had taught me. Oh, how I longed for a day like that. But this wasn't that day. This was a day I would ride in my green mobile destined straight for Hell in a pink dress. This

was the day I would do it. I was certain of that. My thoughts were racing. "Oh God, I don't belong here. Don't they know I am guilty? Don't they know what a sinner I am? There is no way you can forgive me. I must get out of here."

As I walked toward the door, tears streaming down my face, I heard a booming voice "Stop her, don't let her get to that door, bring her to this altar." The Bishop shouted in the microphone from the pulpit, interrupting normal service. I cried harder and harder. I think God must have told the Bishop I was headed to the Second Street bridge, because in that instant, in the middle of testimony service, the Bishop made an altar appeal. The Bishop of Kentucky was the last living Bishop who was appointed by the founder of our Church. He was a Holy-man of God, who was gifted in the Word of knowledge and prophecy. My plan to leave before the altar call hadn't worked. God closed the bridge and made a tolled highway to himself. There I stood at the opening on this highway of forgiveness that would connect me to God. I had no money to pay the toll. I was broken and empty inside. I closed my eyes and heard the Bishop's voice over the chorus of ladies telling me "say thank you Jesus."

"Daughter, God can forgive you, if you ask him. There is no debt Jesus can't pay." In that instant I asked God to forgive me and He did. In that instant, I was bridged into an eternal home, yet plagued by the inability to release myself from the yolk of bondage I placed around my own neck. God had forgiven me, yet I wore a sign over my heart that said, I once did this horrible thing. It took almost twenty years for me to forgive myself.

Twenty years later when I was asked to speak at a Women's conference, I found myself calling for an Altar appeal for those who had attempted suicide. Those who had accepted a false reality. Here I was making the appeal that was made to me over twenty years ago. To my surprise the Altar was flooded with at least fifty women. The assignment was complete, and in just a few minutes I had released myself from guilt and shame. God had forgiven me over twenty years ago and now finally I had forgiven myself. I now know why God had given me another chance. It was these fifty souls that had been tormented by guilt and shame. But, now, they were being freed from pain of their past.

The Bus Stops Here

I sure am glad it's the weekend. *Friday night just got paid!* Who am I kidding? It's not like I have anything to do. I have no car, and to make matters worse I'm making payments for a car I no longer own. It's been a whole year since I was rescued by the Bishop, only to find myself taken advantage of from one man to the next. I guess I am so gullible. I just let my guard down at the sound of wedding bell chime. "I love you." "I want to marry you." Stupid me, I just didn't realize that was code language for I really want to get you in between 500 thread count of white Egyptian cotton. Anyway, I was hurting, feeling ashamed, and felt like the scum of the earth. On one hand, I was smart, pretty, National Dean's List Honor Student, civically responsible, with a nice internship for the summer, thanks to Mr. Franks. On the other hand, I was growing emotionally bankrupt every time I said yes to a smooth-talking lowlife. I was still stuck like Chuck, waddling in the mud. After what happened last summer, Howard, a preacher's kid, and I thought we would give it another try. I even got my own apartment and then I waited on him. I waited and waited; he came a day late and a dollar short. So now I meet the brother of a friend at a party, another preacher's kid. What was it with me and my friend's 'brother's' and preacher's kids? From the word go, I wanted to make a U-turn and run the other way. But this smooth-talking brother had moves. He could sense weakness like a buzzard flying overhead waiting for its prey to die. So, he circled and like a weakling, and I succumbed to a six-month go no-where relationship. It was just another trip down a street that said 'dead-end'. The funny thing is that I saw it coming from the start. I don't know if it was loneliness or sheer boredom that made me travel down that dark dead-end; but whatever reason, I found myself there. It never occurred to me until this moment that this man with initials for a name could be the reason why I'm walking to catch the bus. Mom always had her suspicions and speculation from the beginning. When my car came up missing from his apartment parking lot, she immediately thought he probably sold it for scrap. Now that I think about it, I guess it could have been possible. You never know what someone who wanted to use a Ouija board to win the lottery is capable of. Nevertheless, I reported it stolen, left him and was homeless for two months. I mean I really hit an all-time low this spring semester and got things royally screwed up. All my sorority sisters and friends, except one, had graduated, gotten a job, gone to graduate school, medical school, or law school. Here I was stuck in Louisville and struggling as a result of one bad choice and then another. The only good thing I had going for me was the internship. Now I was back at home, living under someone else's rules. I had to figure out how to make a fast break or something to make a difference. I felt like just giving up. But I only needed eighteen hours to graduate. So after this thought process trickled down regret lane, I fastened my sweater, picked up my purse and left-over donut bag and headed for the bus stop. I normally had the stop to myself this time of day, but to my surprise there was a guest. In the suburbs of Louisville on a busy street there sat a bag lady on the bench. She looked like she had been eating out of a garbage can. Where did she come from? In this nice neighborhood with the finest restaurants and spacious office glass front office buildings, there sat the bag lady. This woman did not fit the landscape of the suburban portrait. I figured she was headed back to her side of town. I had taken the same bus at the same time for the entire summer, every weekday, and had never seen this lady. At first, I just stood there not wanting to make any eye contact with this woman, and certainly not wanting to sit next to the source of the stench that was stinging my nose like an ever-present nuisance, down-right awful smell. I thought about walking the three and half mile walk home or at least a mile and a half to the next stop, but the corns on my baby toes and worn over heels of my pumps that scraped the sidewalk with each step I took, said to me. "Sit down Jacquie, and stop being so silly!" So, I did, and just because I was raised right, I said hello. She looked very intently on the balled-up newspaper she was holding leaning on her fold-up shopping cart she had pulled to the bus stop. When she raised her head, my eyes met hers and I offered her a donut from my bag. They were chocolate covered glazed donuts, my favorite kind. So, this was no small deed, even if I did it just because it was the right thing to do. Her eyes dimly lit reminded me of someone I had seen before. She gently declined, I took a sigh of relief, and as if waiting for opportunity to speak she put the newspaper down on the seat. She looked at me so circumspectly and read my life, and then she spoke. Her voice was strong with a certain wisdom and authority.

"You seem to be perplexed." I opened my life to a stranger. How could she know the thoughts I had just been thinking while walking to the bus stop? I hesitantly replied and tried to deflect her attention from me.

"Yes, ma'am, but I'm ok." Then, ignoring my attempt to cover my true feelings, she spoke words that I would carry in my memory bank that would yield interest for years to come.

She said, "Young lady don't compare yourself to your friends. You don't know how they got what they did. God has a different path for you to take."

The bus showed up and she got on. I nudged my shoulders and raised my eyebrows, a little baffled, and then got on the bus and went to my normal seat in the back. My stop was three stops away before I had to transfer. I thought about what she said. I wanted to tell her thank you. There only two stops in between my stop and where I got on. No passengers exited or got on at those stops so the bus driver kept driving. Normally I would exit the bus from the back, but I wanted to thank her, so I pulled the cord and walked toward the front of the bus. The odd thing is that when I got to the front of the bus, I didn't see her. So, I asked the bus driver what happened to the lady on the bus. His response astonished me. "What lady? Ma'am you were the only passenger to get on." Okay I thought, am I hallucinating? I don't do drugs. I don't eat mushrooms. I know for sure I saw and spoke to this lady.   In my hysteria, instead of waiting for my transfer, took my shoes off and ran barefoot nearly two miles down the street and across the train tracks until I got to my parent's home. My parents had moved back to Louisville after my freshman year of college. No one was home.   I paced the floor back and forth. I could not explain this strange phenomenon. I picked up the phone. I knew MawMaw would be at home doing her favorite past-time this time of day, watching the horse-races. She picked up the phone, "Hellar?" I could tell she had chewing gum in her mouth, Wrigley's Doublemint no doubt. I started in panting trying to catch my breath, "MawMaw, MawMaw, I, I," "She impatiently interrupted, "Jacquenita, Jacquenita, calm down!" So, I said it more slowly but still with a voice of disbelief, confusion, and amazement, "I know this is going to sound strange, but I promise you everything I'm about to tell you is the truth." She paused, "Go ahead on with it." As I recalled everything that happened to MawMaw, she just as matter-of-fact without any doubt summed it up: "That was an angel God sent to warn you. You better straighten up and get right and listen to what she told you. You ain't like everybody else!" So that's it? God sent an angel to tell me that. I guess I always had a knack for doing things my own way. That fall, I moved back on campus to finish my Bachelor's degree.

I am glad I met the old bag lady. I'm glad I went through financial struggle; it made me appreciate and recognize the blessing when I received it. I am glad I went the long route instead of the short-cut to fast money, which is exactly what I was contemplating and trying to justify in my mind. Had I not met the old lady, my life might have just taken a different turn sliding down a slippery slope. I finished college with two degrees in three and a half years and interviewed for a good job with an alumnus of my school. The still image of the woman at the bus was permanently etched in my mind. I could hear her words as if it were an echo. I thought achieving those accomplishments would complete me. I was now twenty and ready to leave Louisville and my mother's house again. This time I would leave with a guide. Early in January I went back to meet with the Bishop of Kentucky in his office. Bishop sat across from his desk and I told him how I graduated and had been interviewing but hadn't landed a job. I was depressed and feeling somewhat worthless. He opened the Bible to the book of James the fourth chapter and pointed to it. "Read it out loud," he said firmly. I read it but I was puzzled. I didn't have two dimes to rub together so how could a scripture on being humble apply to me. As far as I was concerned, I was as humble as I could get. Nevertheless, the Bishop prayed with me and I took that scripture home and studied it and meditated for the next two to three weeks. I began to understand the Spirit of Humility. About 5:00 am on Sunday, January 26th, I cried out to God early. Not like in the past, asking him for stuff. I mean I just started praising him, with my whole being- "*Lord I love you and I need you in my life*." Suddenly, the Holy Spirit of God fell on me. I woke up my brother and sisters unintentionally but unapologetically too. They ran downstairs to tell my parents, and when they heard the noise, I was making my parents reassured by siblings that I was ok. I was finally on the right pathway. I could finally see my destination. It was a journey to eternal life guided by the Holy Spirit. On January 31st of that week, I received and accepted a job offer that commenced my career. Two weeks later I moved to Cincinnati.

DDWD

Don't Drive While Distracted

It has been said that the shortest distance between two points is a straight line. If only life were that simple and you could take the straight line to get to the destination. The journey would be far less unstable and downright frightening at times. It seemed like my path was paved once I accepted Salvation and received the gift of the Holy Spirit. It was at that point distraction was lurking at every corner like a billboard flashing in Vegas that was an invitation to feast on a promising surprise. So, I'm in Cincinnati and driving along very nicely with only a few bumps in the road.   My car was a used Chevy I bought for $500.   For the first three months I bounced around relatives who lived in the Dayton area and commuted in my $500 car back and forth, until I met him.

Surely, he would be the one, he was talking seriously right from the get-go. So, since I had turned my life over to the Lord, I sought out to make my first convert.   We were invited to churches as the relationship progressed. I thought, I don't trust my own judgment. I had made so many mistakes, so I took him home to meet Mama.   I held my breath in the car all the way to church on Easter

Sunday. The silence was broken when Mom asked, "What are your intentions with my daughter?" His response, "Well, uhm, well she has potential." Somebody hit the brakes!!!! Did he just say potential, as if he was shopping in a pet store and deciding which puppy to take home? At least I hadn't invested too much time in him, and when the slightest adversity came, he hit the road. Just like that, Jack was in the wind.

I learned to bring them home quickly. Mom had the gift of discernment. She could tell right away with a handshake the truth about someone. Once she even went on a three day fast just to ask God to lead me away from some preacher's boy who was pretending to be saved. On day three, I called Mom sobbing, "Mom, we broke up, he cheated on me!" Mom just reassured me that he was not the one. Of course, I was none the wiser that she had fasted. Mom did not play fairly.

I guess our relationship had come a long way from the head-strong sixteen-year-old who wouldn't listen to sound advice. She now had me hanging on her every word. I think that made Mom feel good to be my mother. Later that summer we took a trip to Chicago to see old friends and the next year we ended up shopping for hours in the Los Angeles Garment district around 9th and Olympia. We literally shopped so much Mom almost had a heart-attack. While our relationship was on the mend, and I was focusing on work and my career, I still would run into distractions. The danger about driving while distracted is that you might have an accident where you get hurt, or you hurt someone in a crash. The crash could be so bad that you may not even make it to your destination at all, even if you are wearing a safety belt.

So, after a series of near-miss crashes because I was driving while distracted, I decided to focus on my destination. I stopped trying to save every guy I dated. If the man for me was not complete, then he was not for me. I changed my perspective and my focus.

Most of my friends had been out of undergraduate studies at least two years or more and were now starting to get married. Some of them made marriage seem like the only thing you could do, as if it there was no other alternative. It so happened about that time an energizing women's empowerment conference came to town. I had already been single and satisfied for almost six months, so when the speaker pointed me out of an audience of five hundred women, and said, "Daughter, it's your time!" I knew exactly what she meant. I was satisfied being single, going to dinner and the theatre by myself.

Engrossed in preparing to sit for the Certified Public Accountants' (CPA) exam, deep inside I wondered if the man whose rib I held would ever find me. Who was that man for which God created me? Who was the man that I would fit? I stopped going to all parties, even if invited. I didn't think it was inherently wrong to dance or go to a party, but if it didn't move me closer to God or to the man God had for me, I didn't want to do it. The next time, I thought I might talk to a guy, I was going to get to know him on the phone. That's what I did. There were plenty more distractions that looked very appetizing. But I was serious about making it to my destination victoriously.

It was December, cold, and wet, when I started talking to what seemed like a nice young man who had joined our church. After talking to him on the phone for thirty days, in January, I finally agreed to go on a date with him. Imagine my disappointment when I was praying, and God spoke ever so clearly a resounding "NO!"

"No, you may not go out with him!" Teary eyed, I called and canceled the date an hour before he was to show up. This man was so shocked, because he was not used to being stood up.

As if I thought he would believe me, I told him, "The Lord told me that I could not go with you."

He smirked out a laugh, "Well did the Lord tell you when, you could go out with me since I might be your husband?"

"No!" I stated emphatically, "But if and when He tells me, I'll be sure to tell you!"

I hung up the phone, curled up in a fetal position and cried like a baby upset because it had been now nine months since I had been on a date. The need to be hugged or loved, or something was taunting me at the forefront of my thoughts as tears streamed down my face. Nevertheless, I submitted my thoughts to God. I didn't know that I would meet the one I would marry just two weeks later. He would break the mold of my normal stereotype.

Destiny Crossing

"Hey Larue, it's me Jacq. It is 5:00 pm, I turned in the report and put it on your desk for review. I must make it to downtown Cincinnati for the Becker Review course by 6:00, see you tomorrow. "

I was supposed to be in the Tuesday and Thursday class, but it was canceled, so now I will have to settle for Monday and Wednesday. I just finished my prerequisites to sit for the CPA exam last month, so I'm ready. A friend from church and another friend from college will be in the class so this should be interesting, I pondered. As I left work, I changed from my suit into my black size seven jeans on the way. I hated rushing, but I thought I was going to be late. Speeding down I-74, I hoped I didn't get pulled over. Ah, I-75 traffic, what was it with those orange barrels? I exited at Hopple and took Central all the way down. It was 5:55, and I couldn't find a parking spot. Well, I decided to park outside the library, which was even better, because I didn't need to put money in the meter. "Wait, don't close the door, my name is Jacquie Shoulders, I'm here for the class." "It's 5:59, we start on time, hurry and find a seat," the proctor emphasized as he slammed the door closed. Ok, my girl saved me a seat, "Thanks, it's only two seats left out of one hundred and fifty; this class is packed!" I said to my friend from church, catching my breath. The proctor started going through some of the preliminaries, objectives of the class, the syllabus, and house-keeping items. I was so tired from work, I barely paid attention. Then I heard the door squealing open. I can't believe someone is late, forgetting I had just barely made it myself.

"Excuse me, ma'am, is this seat taken?" First of all, I couldn't believe this guy was talking so loudly while the instructor was making his points.

I muttered, "Does it look taken? Sit down, you're late." I guess I could have been a little nicer but after the last encounter with the almost- would-have-been-date in nine months I didn't feel like being courteous to any man. I took the lyrics *"you can't show your teeth to every guy you meet,"* to another level, beyond keeping the teeth and legs closed. The instructor had been rambling, so I looked up at this guy who was annoying me with all his catch-up questions, and I noticed he looked like a friend. "You look like a guy I know named Ben Jordan!" To my surprise, he responded, "That's my brother!" Caution – oh no, another brother of a friend. Even though caution flags were flying, electricity was too! When I went to the bathroom, I could feel his eyes burning a hole in me. I smiled, played it off and gave him the walk! That walk said, "uhm hmm, I know I look good in my size seven black jeans and gold fitted Cashmere sweater, but you couldn't catch me if you tried." Deep down inside I had a feeling that maybe, just maybe he could be the one. But he certainly didn't fit my typical male mold. In fact, he just all out broke the mold. The game was on. One thing I had learned; I would not give him a clue or anyway to know I liked him. He was cocky and confident in a cute way. I liked him a lot! He would have to pass a series of tests.

At the end of class, he approached me just as I thought he would. "So, Jacquie, would you like to study sometimes," he asked? "Yes, I need help in this area of financial statement analysis. Here is my number." I was really serious about the help I needed, even though I hoped it could be more than that. A week passed, and he didn't call. So, after vacillating over it, I told him I joined a study group because I really needed the help. He took that as a maybe she is interested in me. He helped me over the phone with the problem.   The next day was Monday and I had dental work and was very sick from the procedure.   He called to help me but ended up bringing me Taco Bell because the medicine I took made me too drowsy to drive.

Two days later my great uncle Jim passed. He lived in Dayton. We had gone to Dayton every couple of years. In fact, it was my aunt and uncle's house where I went on my first trip at three years old, passing through Cincinnati.   This sparked a flutter of emotions from memory lane with Pawpaw.   The family came up that weekend. Uncle Jim's funeral would be on Valentine's Day.   After the wake, the family from Louisville stayed at my house. The phone rang, my mom answered the phone.   "Oh Jacquie, someone named Jordan, is asking to speak with you." "Ok, I'll get it," I yelled from the bathroom. "So T'nette, what did he want?" my father grunted as soon as I hung up the phone. T'nette was short for my middle name. From the time my father met me, that is what he called me. In fact, he was the only one who called me that. "He wants to take me out on a date, tomorrow, but I told him no because of the funeral. I didn't know if you all would still be in town?" "Jacquenita, you better call him back and accept. You haven't been on a date in nine months. Tomorrow is Valentines! We will be gone back home by 6:00," Mom insisted.

I felt so awkward calling him back after I had just so graciously declined. Maybe he would already have moved on. Maybe not as I went back and forth in my head. As I closed my eyes, I called him back waiting for what seemed like forever for him to answer the telephone. In the back of my mind, I was hoping to go to Benihana. I heard it was nice, but I had never been. He finally answered the phone, and to my surprise, he said he had not made any plans and would love to take me out for Valentine's Day. The next day at 7:30 pm, promptly he picked me up, and he took me to Benihana. Perfect! It was the place I wanted to go, and I hadn't even told him! We laughed and talked all night. We had so much in common. It was the best date ever. He brought me back at 11:00 pm, we shared a quick soft peck in the car, and I walked in the door. I was hooked! "Lord please let this be the one!!!!"

I immediately called Mom and told her about the date since she insisted I call him back and encouraged me to go on the date in the first place. He was still sitting outside in his car when I peeked out of the window. What was he thinking? Later I would find out that he went home and grilled his brother on what he knew about me. His brother told him, "Man don't mess with this girl unless you are serious. My fraternity brother tried to talk to her and she just up and one day called him and said God told her she couldn't go out with him or even talk to him."

The next day I went to work, the whole gang went to lunch, I told them, "I think, he is -" and before I could get it out the chorus led by Larue, finished in harmony "the one!" The awkward silence was broken by the spontaneous combustion of laughter that followed from all of us. "Yeah, the one." I chimed in.

But no matter how my friends teased me, I just kept thinking about the women's conference four months earlier, when the speaker pointed me out and said, "It's your time!" I thought about the prayer I had prayed just fourteen days before he walked into the classroom. I had gone home for Christmas and talking with Mom I shared my loneliness and that I might even move back home. Mom encouraged me to take my request to God in prayer. I had just done that fourteen days before this man walked into the classroom. I thought about the direct order from God not to go out with the man from church two weeks before I met this wonderful man who had just taken me on my dream date. No matter how my comrades teased me, I could feel I was at Destiny Road. It was the pathway ahead in front of me and I was ready to cross the intersection where my street name changed.

I had to be certain. I would not let him know how I felt. I would take this to God before it got serious. The next week I invited him to church. To my chagrin, going into the church, Jordan and the guy I was about to go out with greeted each other. Throughout the entire service, I couldn't focus on what the preacher was saying because of this greeting. How in the world did they know each other I wondered?

Church was different for Jordan coming from a Methodist background. After church he said he enjoyed it. When one of the mothers asked him his plan, I was just ear shy away enough to hear when he told her point blank, "I plan to marry that woman over there." All the single sisters who had crowded around him chimed in in unison. "Whoa, Girl, did you hear that?" I heard him clearly. Clearly, I was more than potential to him. He sounded confident he had found his missing rib. Even though he said that, referring to me, I was not playing. I was not about to make the mistakes I had made in the past. And more urgently I was contemplating how to tell him about the brother at church.

The car ride to the restaurant was a mixture of small talk and awkward silence as I tried to come up with an approach. At the end of dinner, I told him the story of how I had talked on the phone for thirty days with the guy he spoke to, and when we were about to go out, God told me "No, do not go out with him." Jordan sat back and said, "I know you are a woman of God, because you listened to God. If you had gone out with him, I never would have asked you out. I already knew about that because he's my brother's fraternity brother and he has been staying with us."

Wow, I couldn't believe what my ears had heard. How ironic was this? I was relieved and glad now that everything was out in the open. One hurdle was crossed. However, I still needed confirmation from God that he was the one. I no longer needed my mother to fast and pray. I would fast and pray for myself. For three days I took off from work, locked myself in my apartment, and asked him not to call me, because I needed to be sure. When God confirmed through three specific signs that he was the one, I gave that man my heart, and twenty-two months later I gave him my hand in marriage.

We finally arrived at the park in Marietta for my nephews 2nd birthday.   As soon as the car stopped, I woke up.   The kids woke-up too and jetted for the bouncy house. The smile on my sister's face told me she felt so much joy that we would share this moment with her. Although I had missed my sorority sisters, the bond between my blood sisters and I was unbreakable. Even though she tried to come off indifferent, I knew being there meant more to her than sister let on.

The drive to Georgia was only four hours and, in that time, I must have dreamed about my whole life. Naps always made my focus clearer and now we were living life on purpose.

Part II

I Finally Got A Map

Every night for the past few weeks I have had the same dream. First, I start by going over this bridge and back every day. Then I seem to take a drive over a bridge that goes into the ocean. At one point, we are in the state of California, then I am in Japan with my husband and we are inside of these cubes that look like mazes. He leads me in the maze, and then I find my way out of the maze. At the end of the maze we are on an airplane going to Detroit. When we land, finally, we end up at a place buying shoes in Ohio. I kid you not, I had the same dream for weeks. It is so etched in my mind I believe it is a code for things to come in our lives.

Before Google Maps or MapQuest, I remember that the insurance agencies would publish an annual *Road Atlas*. The *Road Atlas* would identify all the state roads, county roads, and interstate roads. At the bottom of the road there would be a legend that defined each symbol on the map. I began to understand as time went on that this reoccurring dream was a road atlas for my life on those things to come. As I figured out each symbol, I still had the undefined parts of the dream etched in my memory.

Thinking back to when I started living life on purpose instead of haphazardly, there seemed to be a driving force of everything going on in my life, my marriage, and job that kept me seeking for a deeper understanding of the things of God and my place in this earth. My husband had always traveled and after having kids I decided to start a business with the intent of working less hours and having the flexibility to be home or on a field trip with my children. They were growing, the business was growing, and my husband, who knew everyone in Cincinnati, was skillfully climbing the Corporate ladder with finesse. We were involved in every community planning event that Cincinnati had to impact the African-American Community, from the Black Family Reunion, Juneteenth, Urban League, African American Chamber of Commerce, YMCA Black Achievers, and I Hear Music in the Air. We were involved with our children's activities, football, dance, basketball, T-ball, and gymnastics. To top it off, we were involved in ministry at the church. We were moving on all cylinders eventually destined for a blow-out from overuse. Then our church started following Pastor Rick Warren's *40 Days of Purpose*. That was the beginning for us to really define what we were doing and why were we doing it.

We led small groups at our home, invited our neighbors and other couples as we collectively unwrapped this nicely packaged method to understanding your purpose. After the 40 days, we went back to our normalcy. Busy was an understatement. Through all the busyness we were thrown curve balls one right after the other. The most challenging I recall, a couple of weeks before my husband went on his second trip to Japan.

September 30, 2004,

"Mrs. Jordan, it's Ms. Kay, I'm calling to let you know that Kevin is very sick. I don't think he is breathing well. Do you want me to take him to Children's Hospital?" I really could not think at that moment. Today, made six years since I had discovered a lump under my right arm – (right axilla), it was also the day of the biggest event I had ever produced, the Faith-Based Financial Training Conference at the Schiff Conference Center. I had somehow gathered almost 500 registered participants, sponsors, and vendors for training and panelists from the Federal, State, and City government. I had scheduled my training classes that I would teach that morning, and we had held our opening plenary session.

Just before lunch I received this terrifying call. I had been training my assistant, Carla, but had no idea that I would need her to step in my shoes and introduce the keynote speaker for the luncheon. Time once again seemed to stand still. I beckoned for my assistant and told her I had to meet my son and the sitter at Children's Hospital. Thankfully, I was less than ten minutes away. Now rushing down Victory Parkway and over to Reading Road and over to Rockdale Street, then Burnett Avenue, I finally arrived in the emergency room. This child's face was nearly blue, is pulse-oxygen level had falling below 90 and he was being admitted to the hospital. That hospital stay lasted five days.

When we got home from the hospital, the water pipe burst in our home causing a flood. The neighbor was able to shut off the water, but the mess it made and the cleanup caused mold to build up which in turn now triggered asthma in my other two children. To make matters worse my husband had to leave to go to Japan. I literally was breaking down. I can't remember how I got through that time with my sanity. I do remember crying a lot and thinking something had to change.

It had been said that without a vision the people perish (KJV Proverbs 29:18). A few years went by and we continued to go through the motions of being busy, until one day we sat down and penned our Vision Statement. I think the downturn of the market in 2007-2008 had a lot to do with us rethinking our game plan. The business was continually growing, but my husband worked in the automotive industry for a company that had never had a layoff. Instead of a layoff, we lost thirty percent of our income from the elimination of overtime and bonuses. We were forced to really look at our activities and what we were doing and why. Through many sleepless long nights and arduous discussion, the Jordan Vision Statement was birthed. Christmas 2008 my husband had our vision statement and family mission framed. This was so significant for our family, our marriage. We had finally written down what we had discussed years before in our *Purpose Driven Life* Bible Study.

Habakkuk 2:2-3 (Amplified) *"Write the vision and engrave it plainly on [clay] tablets, so that the one who reads it will run. For the vision is yet for the appointed [future] time. It hurries toward the goal [of fulfillment]; it will not fail. Even though it delays, wait [patiently] for it, because it will certainly come; it will not delay."*

Now with a sense of living intentional and on purpose we began to submit our plans to God. I remember that following February, my good friend invited me and others to a Warm Spirits sister connect and collaborative. There I completed my first vision board. Within nine months of that vision board, pieces of the vision began to come into play.

Our Vision Statement, Mission, and my vision board began to be my life roadmap. Instead of using my great sense of direction and following signs to get to an unknown destination, I now had a plan and a map to get bring that plan into fruition.

Wheels Up

Ok, I think all my bags are packed. I have a million and one things going on in my head right now. Big Dad is coming so I must make a list for him for the children:

September 26, 2009:

- *Aaliyah and Kevin need to go to bed at 8pm; Michael-Donovan can stay up until 9pm.*
- *The Drs. number is on the refrigerator (she is a family friend and her office is on Galbraith Rd)*
- *Kevin needs to take his medicine for allergies and asthma in the morning and at night*
- *Michael-Donovan and Aaliyah need to take their allergy medicine*
- *Kevin is allergic to Fish, Nuts, Milk, Chocolate, and all Seafood. Repeat Kevin is Allergic to all seafood. His Epi-Pen is in the kitchen drawer.*

My flight leaves in an hour, thankfully we live only fifteen minutes from the airport. Why am I so nervous? I mean butterflies in the stomach nervous. It just doesn't make any sense. I know we agreed that the kids and I would come at the end of the semester, but South Carolina? What do I really know other than my

vacations in Hilton Head? Will the people be friendly?
What about the children? Will I be able to start a
business? All these thoughts at once had my head
swimming, as the wheels lifted-up I drifted off to sleep.

"You will not die on me, you will not die on me," *Boom.*
I felt her hit my back and my chest three times.

 "Ma, I sputtered, it will be ok."

She took out her stethoscope and started screaming at
me – "You are not moving air." Barking orders to my
sister, "Fill up that gallon of water and bring it to me!"

I wondered why mom didn't just take me to the hospital.
She worked at Grady Hospital in Atlanta and had just
walked into her apartment to find me lifeless and itchy.
She raised up the back of my shirt to find I had broken
out in hives.   I told her I was tired and after nursing
Kevin, would just take a nap. Apparently not only her
mother-wit kicked in but her nursing skills.   After
making me drink nearly a gallon of water, she walked
me around her apartment complex up and down the hill.
Wait a minute Mama, I thought you were trying to help
me.   Little did I know, she recognized I had an allergic
reaction to the medication I was on. Kevin was just three

weeks old when I had to have my gall bladder removed. Jordan was on his way to California and didn't want to leave me alone. So, he drove me to Norcross, Georgia where Mom lived. I had been given pain medication that caused my breathing to be shallow. Mom, being a Registered Nurse, sprang into action to prevent another hospital stay, literally pouring water into me so I could pass out all the medicine in my urine. She knows her stuff. It worked miraculously.

The next day she took me to the beach, Tybee Island and Savannah. My Pawpaw was from there, as soon as we passed Hunter Air Force Base, I knew we were close to his hometown. Pawpaw had married MawMaw after she divorced Grandpa Sylvanus. In my eyes, Pawpaw was a hero. Although he never had any biological children that we knew of, he was a good grandfather. He had been gone twenty-four years, but as the smell of the sea became strong in my nostrils and the view in sight, I began to understand his life, where he grew up and even why he left. Savannah was great. As we got closer to the city, I saw a sign that said Hilton Head thirty miles over the bridge. Hilton Head sounded so rich and luxurious. I had heard of this beautiful vacation town, but had never been there. So, I begged Mom to drive us there the next day.   We ended up in Sea Pines at the Salty Dog Café.   I still remember the little beach store where I bought flip flops and a powder blue beach dress. It was beautiful.   We visited the lighthouse and admired the beautiful beach homes.   As soon as we returned to Georgia, I called Jordan and told him all about Hilton Head and that we would have to go there for a visit.

I had fallen in love with Hilton Head, South Carolina and declared that I would one day live there. Indeed, every vacation, every year from that time on was there. As I woke up from my slumber, I marveled that I was now here on board a flight to the Palmetto State. I had researched everything I could about Charleston and this city that would likely be our next home. From the air I could see the shape of the peninsula. We were actually coming into the landing from the Atlantic Ocean. "Flight Attendants prepare the cabin for landing," came over the loudspeakers and I closed my eyes and braced for impact. I hated flying and whether taking off or landing I would close my eyes. With a loud thump and a bump, the wheels touched down and I was about to meet Charleston. As we screeched to a halt and then taxied to the gate, my heart raced as if it was going to jump out.   From time to time in my life, I would have tachycardia, where my heart would race. I think it was primarily from anxiety. This was one of those times. I was anxious to see my husband, whom I had not seen in two weeks. I was anxious about the future and anxious about the present.

The Arrival

Upon arriving to the terminal, I stopped in the bathroom to freshen up and brush my teeth. My husband was supposed to pick me up and I didn't want stinky breath. I planned to smack these juicy lips on his as soon as I saw him. He called me on my cell phone and was running late. I told him that was fine, because the palm trees were gorgeous, and I would just sit there and wait outside. Funny how when you speak things you don't actually think it would come true. When I spoke of moving to South Carolina, I meant Hilton Head, and then I found myself standing in the Charleston airport getting ready to move there. From the time I walked outside I could smell the ocean, see the seagulls flying, and then I saw it, a little green lizard. I could live without the lizards and reptiles, but everything else about Charleston at least at the airport was appealing to the eyesight and smelled just right. Charleston was about ninety miles from pure tranquility. Interrupting my thoughts as I waited for my husband a nice black lady sat down next to me, her name was Virginia. Ms. Virginia's flight had also just landed. Her husband went to get their car as I offered her the seat next to mine.

"You look like your feet hurt," she glared at me.

"Yes ma'am, they do. Your shoes look comfortable," I replied.

"Oh yes, honey, that's all I do is comfortable." She went on to explain to me why. "I can remember I had to have these boots. I wore those boots everywhere. I broke them in washing dishes. Then I had to get help to get those boots off. I had toe problems from then on. I swore I would never wear them darn boots again!" she exclaimed.

I chuckled at her expletives and then noticed she didn't have an accent or sound southern. That's when she told me she had just retired and moved to Charleston and was going to live in Mt. Pleasant after working for the airline for over thirty years in Minneapolis, Minnesota. A few minutes later her husband pulled-up. I thought I would look her up when I returned to Charleston.

Not a bad first impression to Charleston, I thought. The next few days we would take in would be a whirlwind tour of the city, Battery Park, Meeting Street, the Broad Street, SLOB, SNOB, and SOB. That is slightly left, slightly North, and South of Broad references in downtown Charleston. We would go to the beach at Isle of Palms (IOP), taking the IOP Connector. Isle of Palms was just beautiful. Even though it was around 72 degrees, we walked the beach, talked, hugged, and laughed. Something about that beach made me want to live as close as we could while being in a good school district and close to Jordan's job. So, he talked to a co-worker, and got a referral to his wife who was a realtor. She became our realtor and our friend.

We looked everywhere, from West Ashley to Mt. Pleasant, and then back to North Charleston. Sheila and Darrell were from West Virginia; they too were transplants to Charleston. They knew all too well the ways of the South. So, with subtle hints she guided us to make the right housing choice that would be in an excellent neighborhood for the sake of our children and their public education. The apartment complex where Jordan stayed was very close to a very nice neighborhood. I could see myself living there and so it was settled. We would move to North Charleston at the end of the semester.

What a whirlwind weekend. The time had come for me to return to Cincinnati. Heading to the airport I could still smell the ocean saltwater.   We made plans to see each other again in two weeks, meeting halfway in Gatlinburg. This way we could each drive no more than four to five hours and spend the weekend.

As the plane took off for Cincinnati, I drifted off to sleep once again dreaming of the bridges, the maze, and the shoes.

Preparing to Move

After returning to Cincinnati from Gatlinburg it was more and more difficult for our children to say goodbye to their daddy. We were adjusting, but clearly there was a sense of uneasiness. Michael-Donovan became the man of the house in dad's absence. I had to leave him to watch the younger kids while I ran errands, went to the grocery. It was the fall of 2009, and in typical Cincinnati fashion, Indian Summer was in full effect. I tried to keep the children's mind off missing their daddy. On weekends when we did not meet in Tennessee, I would take them to Louisville to see MawMaw, or to Mansfield to visit Grandma and Grandpa.

We went to visit Grandma and Grandpa early in November of 2009 or late October of 2009. At this time of year, the corn fields in Richland County were being harvested. It had been a while since grandpa had gone to church, but he was still a Deacon. Even when we did not attend church, we always had bible study and devotion. On this day in particular, I happened to be teaching my children parable of the wheat and the tare, found in Matthew 13. As I taught the parable that the enemy deliberately sowed tares that were mixed in with seeds planted by God, but at the harvest, God was going to separate his children from those who were not, I peeked Grandpa's interest. Grandpa, hearing me teach, while sitting in his rocking recliner, got his coat, hat and gloves, and whistled to the "Bitties," his great-grandchildren, to follow him out to the field.

We happened to be there on the day the big blue combines were harvesting the crop and clearing the field. He took the kids across their three acres to the back of the field so they could see up close and personal how wheat was separated from tare. I couldn't have taught them a better lesson. Little did we know that would be one of the last life lessons Grandpa would be able to physically demonstrate. Soon after that, his health began to decline.

Later that week, I was talking to my husband and sharing the weekend, when he told me of his own health challenge. Hearing his voice, I got teary eyed, and even though it was only six weeks away, I felt we needed to move right away. There was so much planning to do. I had to appoint a team leader for the office, arrange for monthly meetings and travel back to Cincinnati, contact the realtor, get the house fixed-up, arrange for the movers, get copies of medical and school records. Instead of six weeks, I made it happen in a span of three short weeks. We moved the day after Thanksgiving into a home that we would first rent since we still owned the home in Cincinnati.

Welcome to the South

After driving ten hours from Cincinnati to Charleston, we were tired but finally there. We called Sheila and she would meet us at the house. It was a beautiful home. The living room was open, the family room was open, there was another room that could be a bedroom, office, or dining room and my bedroom was all on the first floor. The colors were a little non-descript but other than that it was perfect. It was just a little more than our house note we were paying in Cincinnati, but with this new job as Director of Internal Audit, we could swing it. It would be tight but doable. We couldn't wait to show the kids their new home or take them to the beach. Each of them would have their own room. The boys would have their own bathroom, plus a guest room and bonus room upstairs. We had driven two cars from Cincinnati, so I was completely tired but excited.

Within minutes of pulling into Cedar Grove Plantation we were greeted with "southern hospitality." The police showed up at our door just as we were unpacking the car and waiting for Sheila to arrive. We were questioned on whether we owned the house. I was somewhat perturbed that the officer felt he could walk in my house uninvited. Stay cool Jacquie, stay cool. When I thought I would lose it, just then Sheila walked in with her southern swag, beautiful blonde hair and showed the officer to the front door. Finally, we had our "free papers". Although I am being facetious, this is what it felt like when the officer left our home. We were free to live in our four walls.

The first thing I found and hung on the wall was our family Vision Statement and Mission. We were in a whole new world with just us. We had to make it and we needed a daily reminder before leaving our safety zone of who we were, what was our vision and what was our mission.

The next day, southern hospitality showed up again with pies and a card. It was from Ms. Susie across the street. The moving truck hadn't even pulled off a good ten minutes.

"Hi y'all doing? I am from across the way and just wanted to welcome you to the neighborhood. I made y'all some pie and cookies.   By the way, I called the police last night, because it was dark, and this property has been vacant since Dr. Morris and his wife moved out almost two years ago, so when I saw someone pull-in at night, I was worried." "Well thank you Susie for coming over and bringing these cookies and pie, I'm sure the kids will enjoy them. Me, I'm on a diet and just ate too much at Thanksgiving," I politely responded.   "Where are y'all from anyways?" she asked.   When I let her know we were from Ohio via Northern, Kentucky, she said, "oh, y'all from up North?" like it was a foreign country.

Just then a lizard crawled in the doorway, and I flipped. Running to get the broom, Susie just brushed it out of the door and when she left, she made sure to tell us to keep the doors closed, since her husband had shot a rattle snake that was wrapped around our mailbox.

As the door closed, I had to go make me some tea and take in all that really had just happened. My neighbor, who had called the police on us brought us food and let us know about the dangerous amphibians and reptiles living in the area. Great, I began for a minute to have second doubts about our little paradise. After all, I had a giant palm tree out front, wetlands outback, I lived twenty minutes from the beach in a seven-bedroom house, it was over 70 degrees outside. The kids were outside playing and quickly making friends. What could possibly be wrong?

As I sat in my chair sipping tea, I drifted off to sleep for a nap. I fell right into the dream picking up in the maze after crossing a bridge. My thoughts were awakened with laughter and loud noises, when my kids came running through the door, screaming, "Mama we went riding our bikes and guess what? We saw an alligator!" My rest was over and so our life began in South Carolina.

There was not much time to relax. It was Saturday afternoon and on Monday, I would have to enroll the kids in school.

Planting Our Feet

Moving to South Carolina took a whole lot of faith. When we moved the scripture came to mind when God told Abram to leave his native country and family in Genesis chapter twelve and go to a land he knew not. We had no family, only each other. We were in a land that really did not take kindly to strangers let alone, northerners. We didn't know their culture or understand their ways. So, we immersed ourselves in the southern culture. After visiting a few churches, we joined Calvary Church of God in Christ in nearby Goose Creek.

My husband was ordained a Deacon at the church and even asked to speak and give a sermon. I became active in the ministry, teaching Bible study, organizing prayer walks, and ministering during the women's day. Jordan began coaching football and baseball. The children were active in school activities and extra-curricular activities. I started a girl scout troop the following summer. I even established a tax and accounting practice for small businesses as a licensed CPA in South Carolina. We did what we could to fit into our new home and surroundings.

It didn't take long for our children to make friends. Before long, our house was hustling and bustling with children. We were now closer than ever to my Mother-in-law who was only four hours away in Zebulon, Georgia. Our home became Jordan Inn where families would come to vacation and enjoy the hospitality and culture of the South. It was an anomaly to me to live in this paradise and not take advantage of the history, culture and richness that it had to offer. Every year for the fourth of July, we would go to our favorite spot at the Isle of Palms and watch the fireworks show over the ocean. This would be our tradition for years to come. We met so many cherished wonderful people.

Eventually, I came to understand the sincerity of my neighbors and appreciated Ms. Susie for looking after the kids and watching for them when they got off the bus if I ran late from meeting with clients. South Carolina had grown on us and we were members of our community that was rooted in the traditions of the South.

I spent many days near the water or at the beach. When Jordan and I just wanted some quiet time, we would go back to the Pier or Battery Park and watch the sunset and dolphins playing and seagulls fishing. Swinging on the pier seemed to ease my mind of everything we had going on. Southern life was very slow-paced. I began driving slowly and taking my time to enjoy life and the essence and beauty of being present. Every time I ventured North for business or to visit ailing family members, when I returned to my home near the sea, I felt peace.

I often visited Isle of Palms or Folly Beach whenever I had a chance. I remember so clearly on Veteran's day I had gone to Tuesday Morning in James Island, which was only two miles from the beach. My grandmother had been sick, and I just thought I would ease my mind with some light shopping. At 11:00 am as I returned to the car, I received a call from my mother, and all she said was "She's gone." Hearing those words felt like a knife pushed through my heart. My MawMaw was my heart. As my mind flooded with emotion, I headed straight up US 17 to the beach. When I got to the beach, I literally rolled around in the sand snot crying. I'm sure the passers-by thought I was deranged. I wasn't crazy but I was hurting. At one point, I thought I heard my grandmother's voice, "Jacquenita, Jacquenita, stop it right now, get up off the ground, and quit-it. I am free, no more pain, I am free." It was enough for me to get up and look around to see who was talking to me. On the 11th day of November, the only thing around was a black, gold, orange, and blue butterfly. I gazed at the butterfly in amazement as it fluttered out into the ocean. This was so symbolic for me to release my grandmother. She was free.

Two-months later, after battling an illness over a year, my grandfather passed away. Our lives became more complexed in South Carolina as we experience heart break and loss. I appreciated being around family more and more each time I was around them.

As our lives became more entrenched in the South, the wear and tear on traveling back and forth to Cincinnati began to surface physically, mentally, emotionally, and financially. The business we had birthed and grown with our hands had flourished in Cincinnati, but the demands of keeping it up began to weigh heavily on me. After my Mother-in-law took ill, she moved in with us briefly. My responsibilities as a mother, wife, and caregiver became overwhelming. It was clear to me that we would need to sell the business in Cincinnati. I shared my intent with my Mother-in-law during our conversation on Monday. She thought it was a great idea because in her words the family would need me more than ever. At the time she said it, I did not fully comprehend what she was saying. Looking back in hindsight, I know she was telling me to be strong because she was leaving to go home. Although we had taken her back to Georgia the month before she passed, I had no idea when I spoke with her on that Monday, that would be the last time we spoke. Within a few weeks I listed the business with a broker, and after three months of due diligence, sold the Cincinnati firm.

The Sisterhood of Matriarchs

With the passing of my grandmother, grandfather, and mother-in-law, I would sit and listen to the Mothers of the church more intently. I was always amazed to hear their wisdom on how they survived and knew exactly how to get things done.

While at Calvary, I was privileged to study under the teachings of the General Supervisor of our International Church. Watching her give advice and resolve conflict was astounding. Her love for the community and her family was evident in that even though she had an international responsibility she still cared deeply for the local community and church. The life-lessons I learned about integrity and character from this well-known, great woman of God, who is respected all over the world, will live on through me. Most of all, she had such a great spirit of humility that has taught me that no matter what your assignment is, it is just that, an assignment, and it does not define you. This great woman embodied what she said, "all of the glory, all of the honor, it belongs to God," with what she did. Thank you, Sainted Mother, for allowing this young mother to sit at your feet and glean wisdom.

There were many other mother figures in my life in South Carolina that were just as precious. Each one of them deposited something great in me. Whether it was learning recipes for meals or just encouragement on how to take care of myself and be a good wife and mother at the same time, it was invaluable.

God puts people in your pathway sometimes for a season and other times for a lifetime. While in South Carolina, I met once-in-a-lifetime friends. You know the kind where you may not see each other often but when you do, it feels like no time has been lost. That's how I felt when I met Leah, Kimberly, and Naomi. Leah and I had daughters that clicked so we spent a lot time with Girl Scouts and at church. Kimberly and I traveled to conventions and would hang out to attend classes. For some reason, most of my friends were always older than me. Most, except Naomi.

Naomi was from the Farrow Islands. I remember the exact Wednesday we met. Jordan was coaching at the middle school, Michael-Donovan was in 8th grade, and it was the first game of the season. Mrs. Jordan, and Mrs. White were assigned to feed the team. Every Wednesday Naomi and I would coordinate meals.

Whenever it was game time, I would look for her and she would be sitting knitting a sweater that could be sold in Macy's. I mean it wouldn't look like my crochet blankets; every stitch perfected with a workmanship and craft that had been passed down from her ancestors to her. After we met, for the next year we had Sunday dinners together. She was the epitome of a Christian.

I was amazed how she planned her annual trip back to Iceland funded with Mary Kay proceeds. Naomi was like my sister from a different mother. We would talk for hours. She always remained true to her own culture but appreciated me for myself. I didn't have to have any pretense. We never talked about our marriages, or work, only the kids and being the best we could be to ourselves. We laughed for hours on end as we attempted the latest diet or fad to lose weight. To Naomi, size, color, and age did not matter. All that mattered to her is that if you were her friend, she was concerned about you. The most important thing in life for Naomi was being present with her kids. She loved being a mom and doing special activities with her kids.

Having settled in South Carolina and assimilated in the culture, this was our home for three years. Just when we were getting comfortable, there was an abrupt change about to occur in our lives. We hadn't shared with our friends or church family just yet what was going on. The war had ended. President Obama was pulling troops out of Iraq which sent the military town in which we lived into an economic quarry. The defense contractor my husband worked for was not immune to the effects. They put in motion a plan to lay-off most of senior management. We had left Cincinnati due to financial crisis from the automobile industry and now we were faced with another crisis. We had just six months of savings, and six months to figure out what was next.

My husband was stressed to the max. Under ordinary circumstances I would have been too. But this time the uneasiness was different. Although the storm was brewing, I had some peace of mind. I had reassurance that God would take care of us. I rehearsed our Vision Statement over and over in my mind. I remember telling the Lord, "I don't know how you are going to get the Glory out of this, but this I know you will get the Glory." But I would be remised if I told you there wasn't a moment that I briefly felt like we had been brought to South Carolina and we had failed. Whatever doubt I had to swallow it or put it in a bottle and let it drift out into the ocean. I had to believe that "we are the evidence of God's faithfulness." There is no way he could lead us here to fail. Believing that and going into my prayer closet, it was time to take the foot off the gas and put on the cruise control. It was time to put down my map and tap into a higher technology, my GPS – God Provision System!

Part III

My GPS Works!

Re-Routing, Recalculating, and Recalibrating

After the bomb-shell news we received, reality was sinking in fast. Spring was coming soon in Charleston, that meant the trees would be mating, and everything would be green. Literally tree pollen would float through the air. When you blew your nose or cleaned your ears, a yellowish dew would be present. This meant Kevin would need more medication to keep from getting sick. The last pay day was the last Friday and day of February. On the first day of March, Kevin woke up wheezing. After twenty minutes on the nebulizer I decided we needed to go to MUSC Children's Hospital. This child was in bad shape and for the second time in his life he was admitted to the hospital for an extended stay, a week and a half to be exact.

This was either the worst timing in the world or the best timing. Our health insurance had expired the day before, but we were within the window to purchase COBRA insurance which we picked up the very next business day. It was worth paying to avoid the twenty-thousand-dollar hospital bill that we were about to be hit with.

To make a little extra money, I picked up additional clients and began looking to go back to work. I had three call backs for a GS-15 level at the Department of State. I interviewed for a Team Leader position with the Department of Veteran Affairs. These jobs all seemed promising, but my husband would also need a job. He had several promising interviews but nothing stuck. It had been two and a half months since the lay-off took effect. Our oldest son was leaving for Paris and Barcelona a few days before spring break for a school trip he had funded himself through candy sales and donations from family, friends, and our church. I thought it would be a good idea if we just got in the car and started driving toward Cincinnati. We could stay with family and friends; we really only needed the gas money to take us there and bring us back. My husband, looking at the budget, did not want to make the trip. Finally, he agreed that we could go. At least seeing family, we could get strengthened in our family bonds, we could laugh again. It would be as refreshing as the sunshine comes after a storm has passed.

"Jacquie, Jacquie… wake up, wake up," Jordan had this perk of energy in his voice I had not heard in months. "Hmmm, what, what is it? What's the matter," rubbing my eyes and clearing my throat. We had been driving for a little over three hours when he got a phone call as we were crossing into North Carolina. "I just got a call from a guy who wants to interview me in Detroit." All I heard was "interview" and when I asked him when, he said day after tomorrow. I was like let's do it. "Ok that sounds great, we can drop Kevin and Aaliyah off in Mansfield and we can drive to Detroit from there, it's not too far from Toledo."

We were on our way through Knoxville to Cincinnati when we got the call. Now we were going to go up I-77 instead of I-75. Our course was re-routed just like that. On the way home after the interview, not really knowing the outcome of the situation, we stopped by our former Bishop's house to say hello in Toledo. We had been part of his fellowship before we moved to South Carolina, so if we were possibly coming back this way, it was quite natural for us to stop by and apprise him and his wife of our situation.

As we headed to pick up the kids in Mansfield, Jordan got another call. This time, there was an interview in Cincinnati. So, we headed South down I-71 and stayed in town a few days. I often marveled at just how precisely accurate the breakthrough for us was. At every turn in our circumstance, we simply had to trust that God would work it out. The more we were able to trust God, the less we worried, and the more God proved that we were indeed evidence of his faithfulness, love, and power. God was working overtime behind the scenes to set us up for what was next.

We headed back to South Carolina full of hope. It was mid-April, and spring break was coming to an end. We would pick up our oldest son from the airport on Sunday. We still hadn't told anyone about what was going on with us. A month passed by and we were now in May, still no word on the job and not an offer in site. By May we had shared our situation with the Bishop at Calvary. We never wavered in our financial giving to the church, as stewards we invested our time, energy and resources into people and things that yielded fruit.

Later in May, Jordan finally heard back from the company and they wanted him to start in Michigan within two weeks. As we had before, he would go ahead of the family. School would be out soon, and we toyed with the idea of the family staying in South Carolina, as Michael-Donovan had been practicing football at the high school with one of the legendary coaches. However, I quickly changed my mind after visiting in late June. With the help of my Aunt Brenda, and our realtor Sheila, we prepared the house to go to market in just three days. We packed up the car and left South Carolina just after school was out. We weren't up North seven days when I received a call from Sheila letting us know we had an offer on the house and it was for more than we asked. We accepted the offer and closed on the house in less than thirty days.

We would spend one last Fourth of July with our South Carolina friends before leaving for Michigan. Our annual pilgrimage to Isle of Palms had become such a tradition that even our native friends began to visit for the fireworks show. We would come back for the next several years between Christmas and the Fourth of July.

Beyond the Bridges

"Babe, what are you humming?" Jordan asked me as if he had never heard the song by Simon & Garfunkel. "When you're weary, feeling small, when tears are in your eyes, I'll dry them all (all) I'm on your side, oh, when times get rough and friends just can't be found, like a bridge over troubled water, I will lay me down, like a bridge over troubled water I will lay me down." "Babe, wow that is so sad," Jordan went on to say. I did have a flare for the dramatic, but that is just how I felt. Here we were traveling over the Arthur Ravenal Bridge heading to our last Fourth of July as residents of South Carolina.

Naomi and her family were just in the car behind us. It seemed unreal at times that I had only known her for a year and how close we had become since the first football practice last summer. I just didn't want to leave that feeling of love and camaraderie; she was my sister. Not to mention, I was connected to Kimberly the designer and party planner extraordinaire who had become my friend and Leah who was always there to lend a helping hand. True friends are rare and once in a lifetime and I just didn't want to leave that all behind.

I closed my eyes and soaked it all in, took a deep breath and exhaled. When I opened my eyes, it was like a bright light shining and for the first time since I had the reoccurring dream in 1998, fourteen years later I understood. "Jordan, Jordan, I get it! I finally get it!" I was so excited to share my epiphany. Jordan was so used to my deep revelations. He just waited calmly for me to explain. "You know that dream I have been having for years, I finally understand. When I would be driving back and forth over this Bridge, that was me taking the kids to school in Avondale and then coming back every day to Kentucky. But then the dream would change, and you and I would be in this maze in Japan. I figured out that the maze was you working for Toyota, although I am not sure why I was in the maze. The other part of the dream is that we would be driving as if going straight into the ocean, that is here!" Just then we topped the crescent of the bridge on the IOP connector and all you could see was the ocean, for a moment it looked like we were driving straight into the ocean. The other part of the dream is that we would be going to Michigan, and ironically here we were moving to Michigan.

I still didn't have revelation on what shoes in Ohio meant or me in the maze in Japan, but at least I understood part of the dream. It was a roadmap for our lives and God had put his GPS in my mind's eye and let me see a glimpse of where we were and where he was taking us. I could at least breathe in knowing that wherever we were going God was taking us there. How else could we explain the house selling in just seven days? How else could we explain the job interview when we simply took a leap of faith and started driving toward the North during spring break? It was God moving us. God was carrying us and wherever he was moving us his provision would be there. As long as we followed the Glory cloud, we would get to our destination safely.

The dream was finally revealed in part fourteen years later. I would no longer be plagued with anxiety trying to figure out the meaning of this dream. Fourteen was a sign of deliverance. From my bible study I remembered that Paul and Silas were shipwrecked fourteen days. I remembered that Joseph was imprisoned fourteen years. I was glad I could take a deep breath being reassured that God makes no mistakes and every turn we made he was carrying us every step of the way.

The process of moving from South Carolina was much different than moving to South Carolina. We owned the house in Northern Kentucky for nearly two years during a terrible housing market after moving to South Carolina. On the opposite end of the spectrum we sold our house in South Carolina as the market was turning around. We seemed to be picked-up on a magic carpet and deposited in Michigan. The children were able to finish out the school year in South Carolina, so it was not as abrupt of a move before the end of the semester, as we had done moving to South Carolina. It was a strategic and pivotal move for all our children. Although Aaliyah would not be able to attend the School of Performing Arts that she had auditioned and gotten accepted into, she would get to try something new. Kevin would enter school with more resources than ever, and because the air was crisper, his breathing improved. It was the start of high school for Michael-Donovan and he would benefit tremendously in football and wrestling by being in Michigan. Overall, while it wasn't our first choice to move, we followed as God led us to our greater, from our desert place to our Oasis and it happened to be in Michigan.

Imprints from the Holy City

Reflecting back to the first time I heard of Charleston, I had to look it up on a map. I read as much as I could about this city. The Holy City it was called, and I wondered why a city whose skyline was lined with church steeples attended by people devout in their faith could justify its place in history. Charleston culture was the epitome of everything the book said and more. It was steep in history and culture, exquisite southern cuisine perfected on the age-old recipes of slaves and former slaves. What I saw in Charleston was a city that held on to its traditions while keenly aware of its sins against humanity. The markets where slaves were sold and the dungeons where they were kept chained still stood as a memorial of its painful past. Charleston, in my eyes, was a city so desperately trying to move into the future, but with one foot on the gas and one foot on the brakes. I couldn't understand how the oppressed and the oppressors could live and coexist in separate worlds, but there were unwritten and unspoken rules that everyone seemed to follow from religious, political, and community affairs.

Aside from reverence and homage to traditions, I found if you really got to know an individual personally you found out that they were just down home and down to earth. They were genuine. They genuinely liked you or they genuinely didn't. Either way, there was no pretense and you knew it. There were no two-faces. Only one face was shown, and it said I will prejudge you based on my experience until I know you. It helped me to realize that everyone has implicit bias, which will cause them to prejudge. However, when that implicit bias causes us to impart justice differently, hire differently, or worship differently, then I believe we have crossed the line.

I grew spiritually while in Charleston. I learned and gleaned so much from the church we attended. The church we went to sang hymns and even sometimes we had Gullah Christmas program. I loved singing the old hymns. We didn't just sing the refrain of the hymn; we sang the entire four or five verses of the hymn. The hymns told stories of survival and victory, and how to win by faith and trust in the Lord. Some hymns were sad, but others were joyful. They were all praises to our Almighty God. In our modern charismatic era of Christendom, the history and purpose of hymnals has become extinct. Many of the hymns were scripture verses explained in Psalms, Proverbs, or Lamentations. Praise and worship has its place in adoration to God our Father, and his spirit often moves during those services, but every now and then we need to reflect on where we are, where we have been, and where we are going.

When I started writing this book, I thought about my journey and what it took for me to get to a place spiritually to learn to respond to the stimuli in every circumstance with prayer and faith instead of reacting with fear. I thought Charleston would be the place I would retire and live the rest of my days collecting shells on the beach. In Charleston, I had no choice but to slow down and enjoy the relaxed atmosphere. In hindsight, it was more sojourning to a temporary place in life, rather than a journey to a destination. Charleston taught me how to deal with loss and pain and then to keep moving forward toward living and not just existing. In Charleston, my children met lifelong friends and that defined them. If you ask them, they will tell you they grew up in Charleston. In Charleston, they found friendship and stability. No more were we going back and forth across the bridge to school and church to worship in a neighborhood away from their home. For the first time in their lives they rode a school bus. For the first time in their lives, for the most part their mom was home when they arrived at home. For the first time in their lives we worshipped not far from where we lived. Charleston for them was a security blanket. They weren't totally oblivious to the ways of the South. They heard their dad talking about the tickets and being pulled over at least once every other month for seemingly no reason at all. They witnessed the dangers of the swamp when their dad ran over an eight-foot rattle snake. They witnessed the black and yellow garden spider that made a camp in my bedroom window. They understood the history and culture of Charleston even more so than I did because it was relished and taught in the school system. They would come home and share their experiences with me. "Mama – black and yellow, kill a fella, but red and black, you're ok, Jack." It was Kevin who immediately recognized the venomous spider that made her home in my bedroom window. Life for them was not without challenge, but their mom and dad traveled less, and we were able to really enjoy our home and being together.

A holy city is a sacred place, and for what we learned from our brief stay, Charleston was that for us. It further shaped our minds, mended our hearts, and deepened our faith in God.   In Charleston, our vision as the evidence of God's love, power, and faithfulness was actually manifested in our relationships with each other, our worship and our stewardship.

Life has its twists and turns, and we have to adjust, respond, and react to what it gives us. Recently I had the opportunity to visit Italy. I recall being in Ivrea, Italy taking a bus trip into the city that was only four kilometers from my hotel. After shopping and lunch, I boarded the bus to journey back to my hotel only to find that I had taken the wrong bus. On the bus ride back, the scenery was so beautiful, that I didn't realize it was not the way I came, until we were headed up the mountain. At that point, anxiety began to set-in and I thought, "Uh-oh what have I done?" Not knowing what was up ahead, I began to pray. God responded in a gentle nudge of reassurance that he would take care of me. When we got to the top of the mountain the bus driver decided to take a break. This meant I would have to get off the comfortable bus in an unfamiliar city, with no cell phone use, no one who spoke English, and wait patiently for his one-hour break to be completed. This was an unplanned, unexpected detour. I hoped this bus excursion would come full circle and take me back to where it had picked me up. While waiting, I thought about how leaving Charleston had been an unplanned, unexpected move to Michigan. In that moment I knew that no matter the twist and turns, no matter the detours in life, or how far off the beaten path you may go, it only takes a nudge from God, faith in his plan to turn it around, to bring you back to the place where it all began. When you come full circle, you come back "full", wiser, with greater knowledge and understanding of your purpose. While on that mountain top I reflected my life and how in my early younger days I didn't know I had a map or a GPS, I simply followed signs or clues on what was next. When I figured out that a vision gives you direction on what's next, that became my roadmap. Again, it was my "Vision." Now I am in a place where God takes me, I will follow, where he leads me, I will be alright. I even know as my children make choices, mistakes, and set out on their own journey God will be with them as He has been with me. I am stronger! I am wiser and I am ready for what's next.

Appendix
Book Discussion Questions

1. What was the turning point in the author's life that helped her find her way?

2. What role does forgiveness play in helping one identify their purpose?

3. What are the ways that God can speak to or through an individual? Give examples as evidence or support.

4. What current circumstance or memory of a situation is keeping you from moving forward?

5. Are you using tools to navigate your own personal journey? If so, what are they and are they effective?